BREATH BURNS AWAY

RAYMOND MCNIECE

IMAGES BY TIMOTHY LACHINA

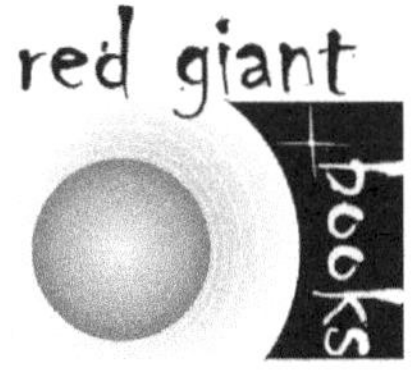

Designed by Timothy Lachina

AMERICAN STYLE HAIKU AND SENRYU

Many of the poems in this collection are not haiku in the strictest sense. Yes, they are composed of three short lines in the present tense releasing a moment of revelation — outsight insight — in short, a verbal rendering of the "aha" moment of zen awareness. And they often depict that intersection between human and nature. But they do not employ a 5-7-5 syllable format which is, anecdotally anyway, the first response for a layman's definition of the form. Nor do they have a "kigo", or season word – in traditional Haiku one word from a set list to denote the time of year in which the poem occurs, for instance "frog" for spring. Neither do they use the "cutting" word, a verbal particle to accentuate the juxtaposition of images which usually occurs at the end of the second line; although they do occasionally use a dash to that effect. Many of the poems here could be called senryu, comic haiku that describe incidents of human nature.

I feel compelled to mention this to warn off purists' criticisms. These are American English haiku/senryu. I make no claim otherwise. Those seeking traditional Haiku should learn Japanese and peruse the copious lists of "kigo" that a highly formal and ritualized literary tradition (based on Chinese models) created over centuries. But bear in mind that Basho, the poet most identified with haiku, upended that very tradition in many of his latter haiku — the famous frog pond haiku being an example of that.

These are haiku and senryu in an American style, more akin to Kerouac's beat "pops", Richard Wright's efforts, and Robert Hass' translations of the big three — Basho, Buson and Issa. Some haiku herein hew to the aforementioned formats, while others are aphorisms, imagist collages, short short narratives, and even jokes with a set-up/ set-up/ punchline structure. They are influenced by my zen studies and my own idiosyncratic interpretation of the form. They are a direct response to a moment, be that moment in nature, from reading the news, or a passing thought, with the technique of "notice what you notice" and get the ego out of the way as much as possible. They are not about capturing that moment, but realizing it and releasing it on breath — breath which is nothing but the basis of the universe.

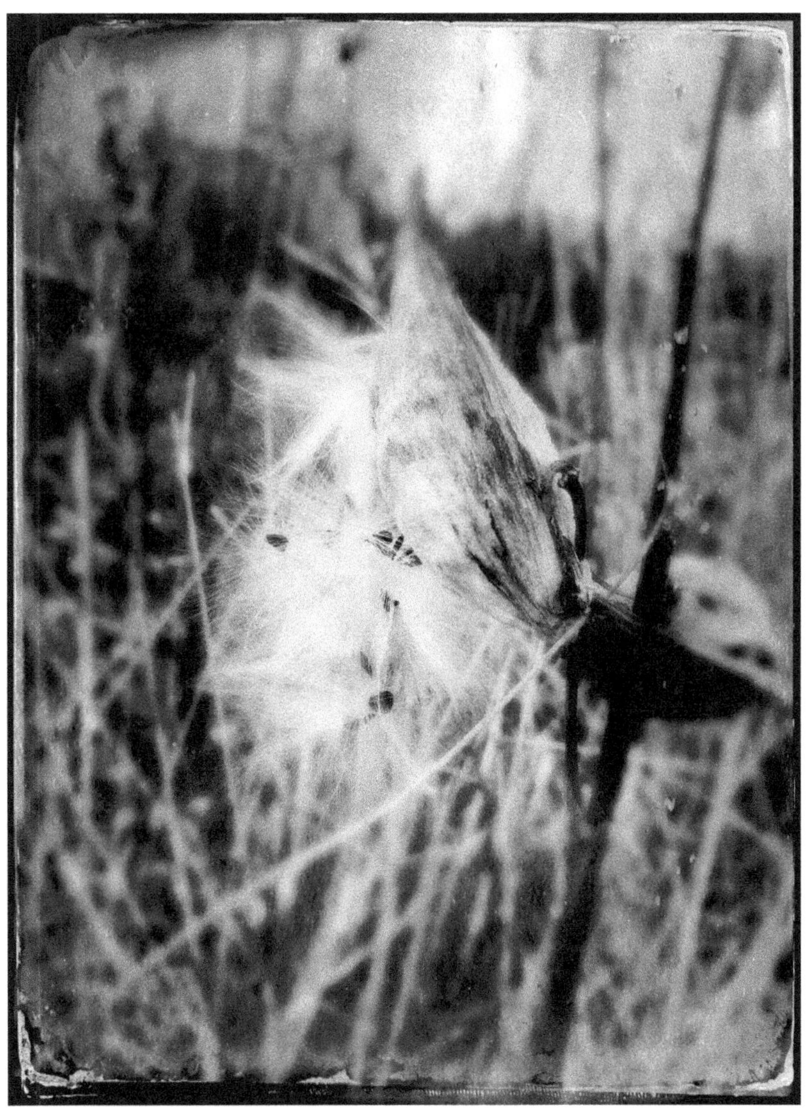

O N E

RIPPLING TOGETHER

office windowsill,
fly poised for flight
three months now

morning flurries
web sac of shriveled flies
between window panes

waxing moon,
wine bottle
almost empty

cold fall puddle —
bare branches and my face
rippling together

crickets sing tonight
between rush of traffic,
this breathing

ant walks my shoulder
as I sit by the road,
far from home

old Joe stray dog
flops down bad hips on mattress
still warm from my bones

lifting fly from stream,
gleaming wings –
spring sunset

leading under truck
muddy pawprints,
cat's haiku

white heron's stare,
camera click –
golden eye

dead Xmas tree
on curb, empty gift box
filling with snow

spider web
spans odometer
thousands of miles

sitting –
not even the same silence
comes twice

cricket antenna
pokes from sidewalk crack,
traffic rushes by

it took eight years but
identical snowflakes were found,
melting out of sight

last live cicada
clinging to broom handle,
I sweep husks off deck

lengthened icicles
dripping quickly –
aching bones

bass leaps from stream
flashes through dusk
until moment of death

web stuck on face –
spider, I've ruined your house,
I spit out your lunch

tide comes in –
fish eating ants that feasted
on dead fish

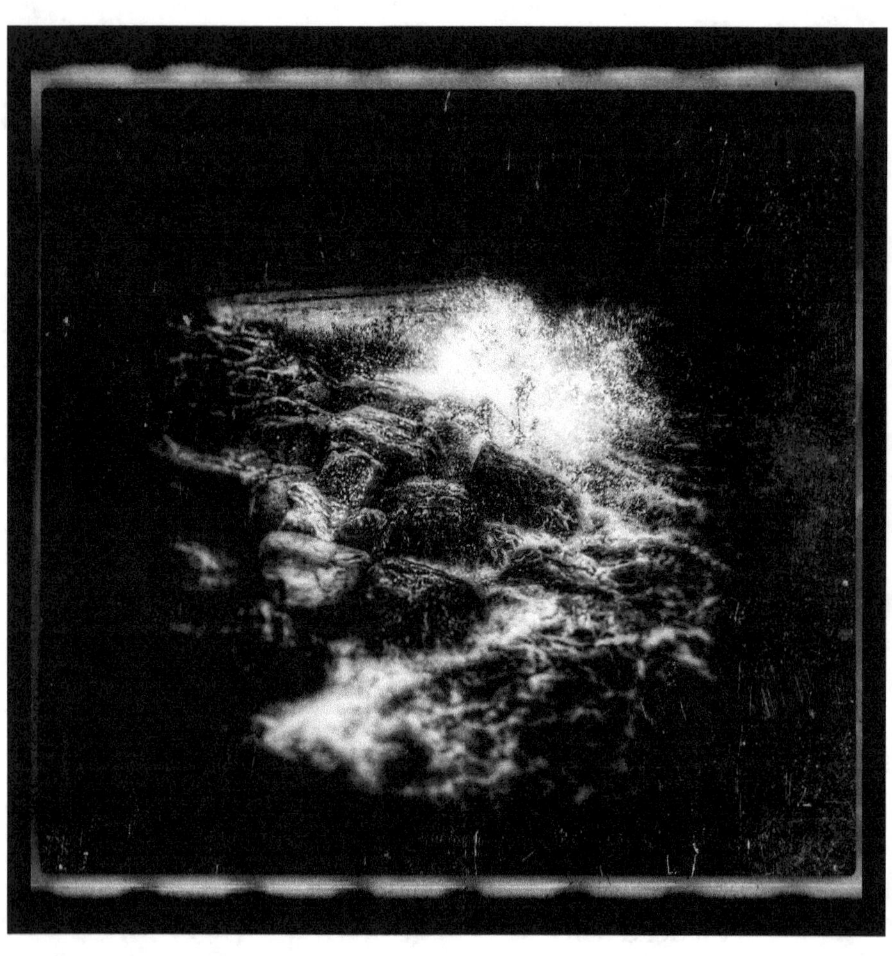

SIX

afternoon ocean
dreams an ocean and wakes
into waves

one thought expands —
basho's frog pond *plop,*
stars scattering

recreating basho,
she throws a stone in pond,
her arms rippling

suburban lawn
whirring of weed whackers –
cicadas

sea's song too vast
to hear unless shell
is held to ear

tarpon scale
held to sun –
liver spotted hand

head bent looking
for ancient shark teeth –
sunset surf

half moon on stream bed
will not wash away,
moon beams pulsing

leaf matted pool
reflects grey November sky
around lined face

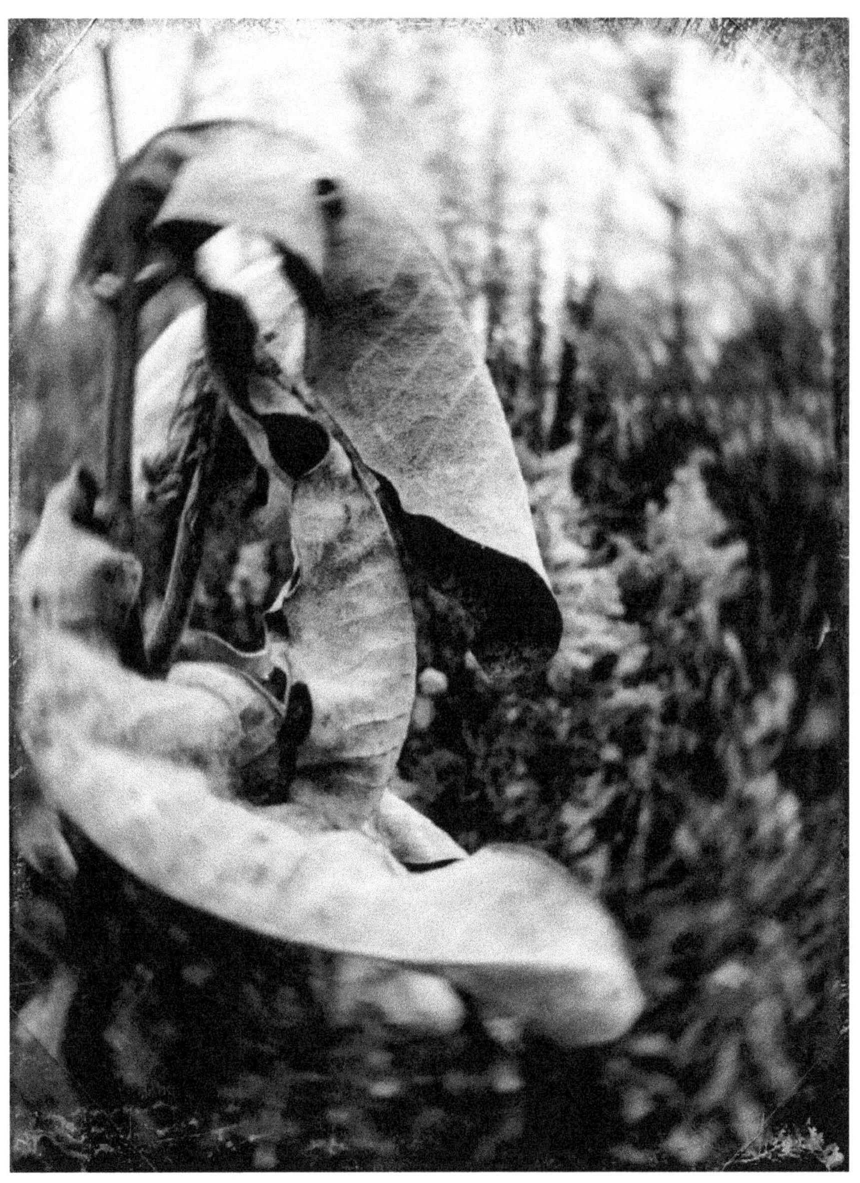

NINE

YOU, ME AND THE FULL MOON

Not face book, face screen —
when we're really face to face
we see eye to eye

fake news meme
algorhithms —
IN-YOUR-FACE book

Visayas road dusk –
every flower reminds of you,
gumamela lips

we're getting down,
butt naked menage a trois,
you, me and the full moon

dead sparrow on sidewalk —
the bones of your hand
once fit into mine

full moon
writing a haiku,
fingers on her back

I'm still a hot babe
she says, *it just comes*
in flashes now

kissing in the dark
to memorize your face
the morning I leave

she tries to smile when
I hold the door open —
black eye swollen

older now than dad
when he died, inheriting
his unlived years

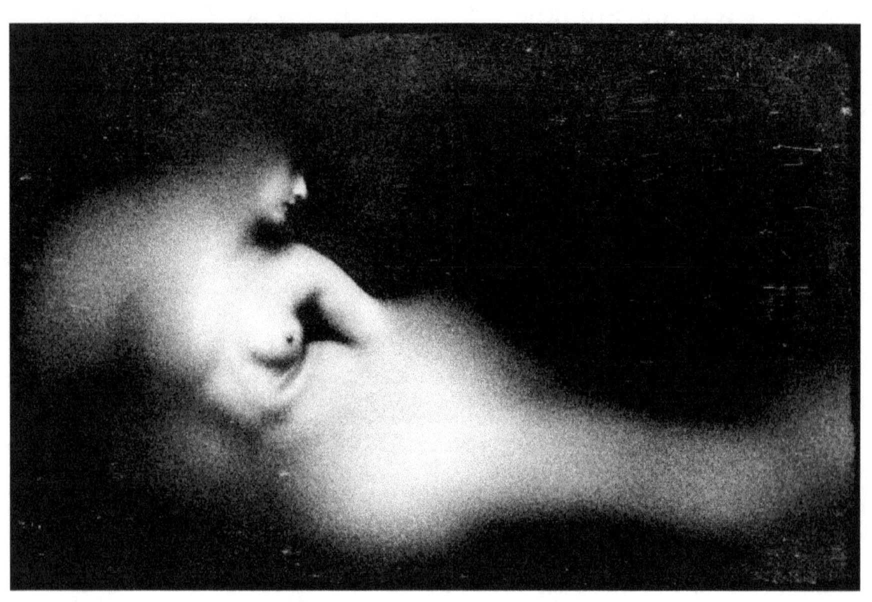

TWELVE

she calls from Cali,
you got a big one but it's not
1,000 miles long

cupped in empty nest,
the first light of the snow –
you still in Cali

Christmas present,
my last full Vicodin
for busted sister

wanna die making love,
coming and going
at the same time

hollow stump
initials carved in heart,
eaten by bark

my sister's hands
on back of folding lawn chair,
her budget walker

she tells me to pitch
or get off the mound, so I take
my balls and bat home

our bodies coming
together, tuned to O –
home note of love

after lovemaking,
the dying black cat
wheezing last breaths

Neolithic couple
unearthed, skulls touching,
whispering dust to dust

showering together,
watching monsoon bamboo
swaying May wind

all night ice sliding
off the roof — beside me,
your soft breathing

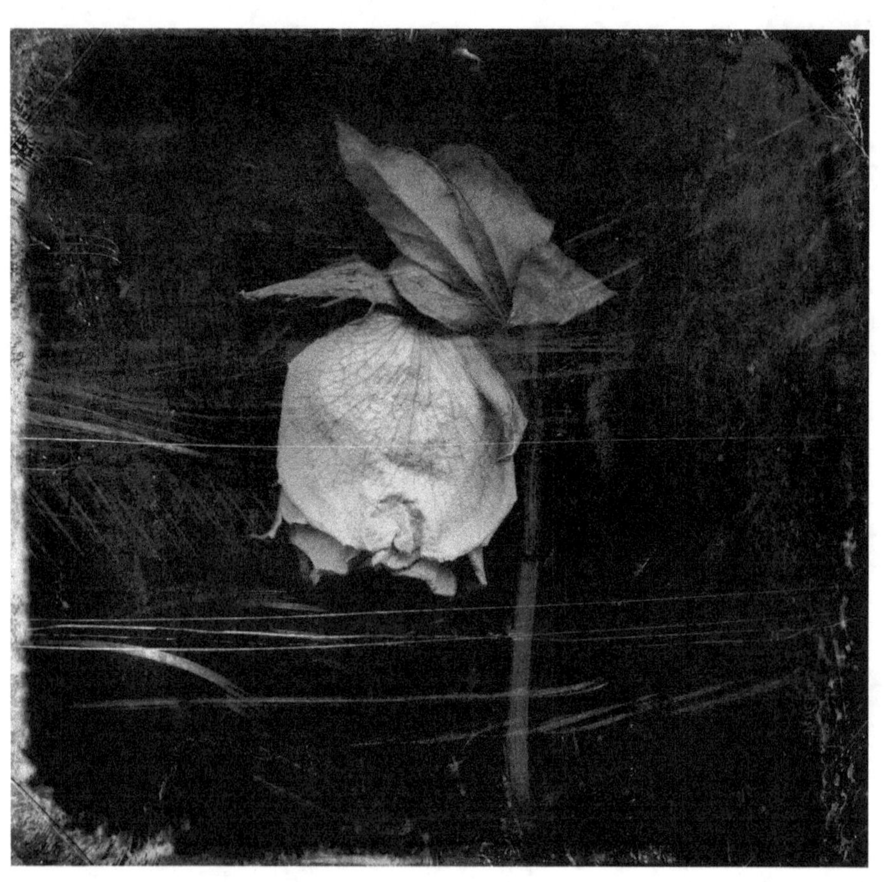

SIXTEEN

AS MANY BULLETS AS TEARS

more suicides
than casualties
in the Afghan war

the world is dying
for a one dollar burger,
unhappy meal

that drop of heroin
taking Zak all the way back to
Afghan poppy field

church fundraiser:
AMMO FOR JESUS to help families
of gun violence

It took 800 years
for the Roman Empire to fall —
they didn't have internet

blessed are the meek?
Jesus gonna kick some ass —
he only has two cheeks

global warming,
Inuit don't have as many
words for snow now

trickle down system,
the rich pissing on our backs
and calling it rain

the first language
was numbers, the first numbers
were slaves

America, as many guns
as people, as many bullets
as tears

paint ball fort in park,
over in Afghanistan
my nephew on patrol

Jesus said we should love
everyone —he did not say
we have to like them

the Union won
the Civil War but the south
won the government

foreign policy —
we'll bring democracy
if we have to kill them all

how big is our flag?
big enough to cover all
those dead Iraqis'?

Disneyland motto,
Happiest place on earth,
registered trademark

here lies America's sex –
caught between puritans
and pornographers

if black folks got it
so easy, why not
trade places with them?

museum silver doubloons
should be red for all the blood
shed to coin them

immigrant baby
bobs along shore – not enough tears
to wash away shame

South Carolina back road
rusty pole confederate flag,
white sheets on clothes line

fracking the earth –
the world won't end with a bang,
just multiple farts

earth six thousand years old
deemed a correct answer on
Kentucky school test

green numbers flicker
stock market screens –
forest fires out west

tallest pyramids
are banks, built grain by grain,
deserts spreading

racism isn't worse,
it's just being videoed
by citizens now

America, your pursuit
of happiness runs through empty lot
to the dollar store

coffee mug made at camp
found in Twin Tower rubble,
World's Greatest Mom

Sandy Hook shooting –
just another ricochet
from Afghanistan

plastic dinosaur
kids ride in the playground —
extinction oil

as many plastic beads
in the sea as stars in the sky —
cancer universe

PLACES, CLEVELAND

Cleveland winter,
I shovel the lawn
just to see green

Cleveland winter,
grey lid over cold oatmeal
stuck in back of fridge

grandma says, *never*
put your winter coat away
in Cleveland

none can still speak
Cuyahoga river tongue,
Erie tribe long gone

two straight weeks
of Cleveland grey skies,
mother's milk for locals

TWENTY-FOUR

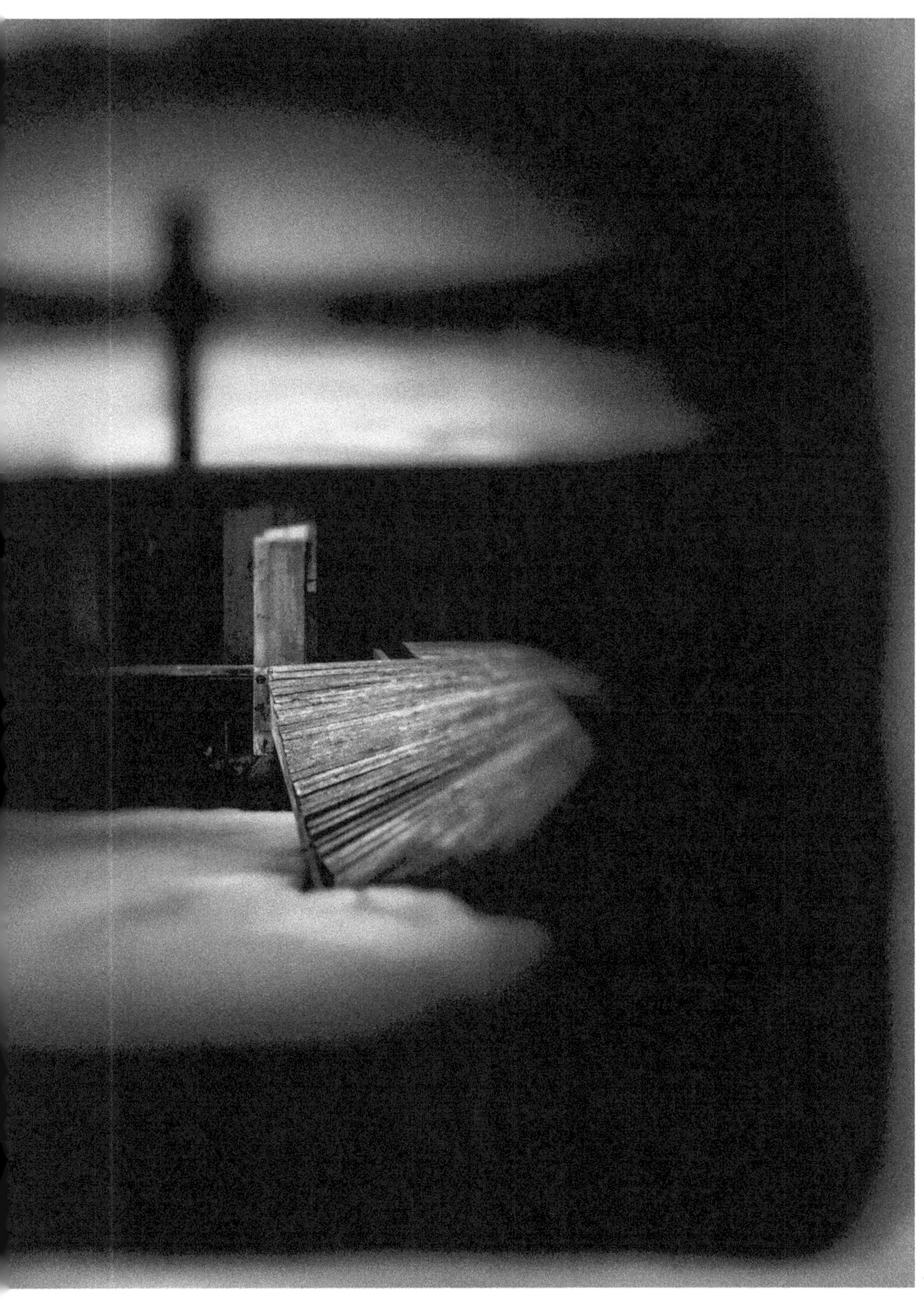

TWNETY-FIVE

Cuyahoga dawn –
burning river running through
this rusty heart

Cleveland winter skyline –
city's secret motto,
rust never sleeps

pole at wharf's end
etched with lover's names
rusting

Moses cleaved
the Cuyahoga, left his name
to THE LAND

spring pothole season
blooming Cleveland streets,
blue sky puddles

blue flame steel mill stack
rising over Cleveland's flats
eating this blizzard

Lake Erie sunset –
baked brick, CLEVELAND BLOCK
worn by blue-green waves

Lake Erie fish blood
pools granite pier block,
sticky sunlight

Lake Erie wave crash
splats on notebook page
haiku blurs blue

hurrying to snap
spring equinox sunset photo,
I slip off jetty

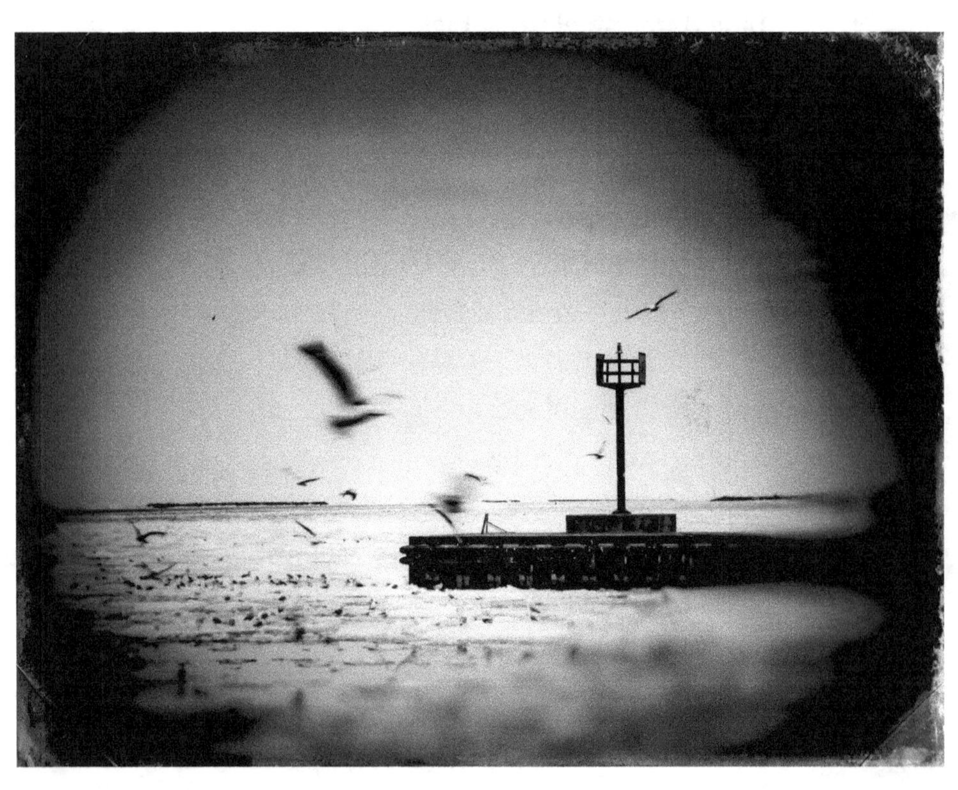

scabs of crusty snow
melt from blanched lawn —
Cleveland remains

gulls squatting ice floe,
beaks stropping flopping shad –
bloody ice sunset

black steel bridge points
skyward through unpolluted sky,
workers gone like smoke

East Cleveland evening –
foreclosed eyes of bandos,
neon LOTTERY sign

Driving potholed street,
a sign missing an 's' reads
Cleveland ( )crap

SPRING TANKA, CLEVELAND

Floating on spring breeze
shredded blue plastic bag
flutters in the branches
amidst swirl of cherry blossoms,
ragged clouds across azure sky.

Grey clouds off the Lake,
grey faces of skyscrapers,
one yellow daffodil blooms
from rust flakes and cinders
glinting Cleveland gutter.

Dump truck spills gravel
into a cloud of dust
back hatch clangs and clamps,
new oak leaves shine
light green flames.

Crab apple blossoms blow
along MLK Boulevard
hip hop beats bump through traffic,
everywhere you go today
windows down, spring opening.

Apple blossoms swirling
through May Day breeze
settling atop museum lagoon,
traffic on Euclid Avenue
crunching winter cinders.

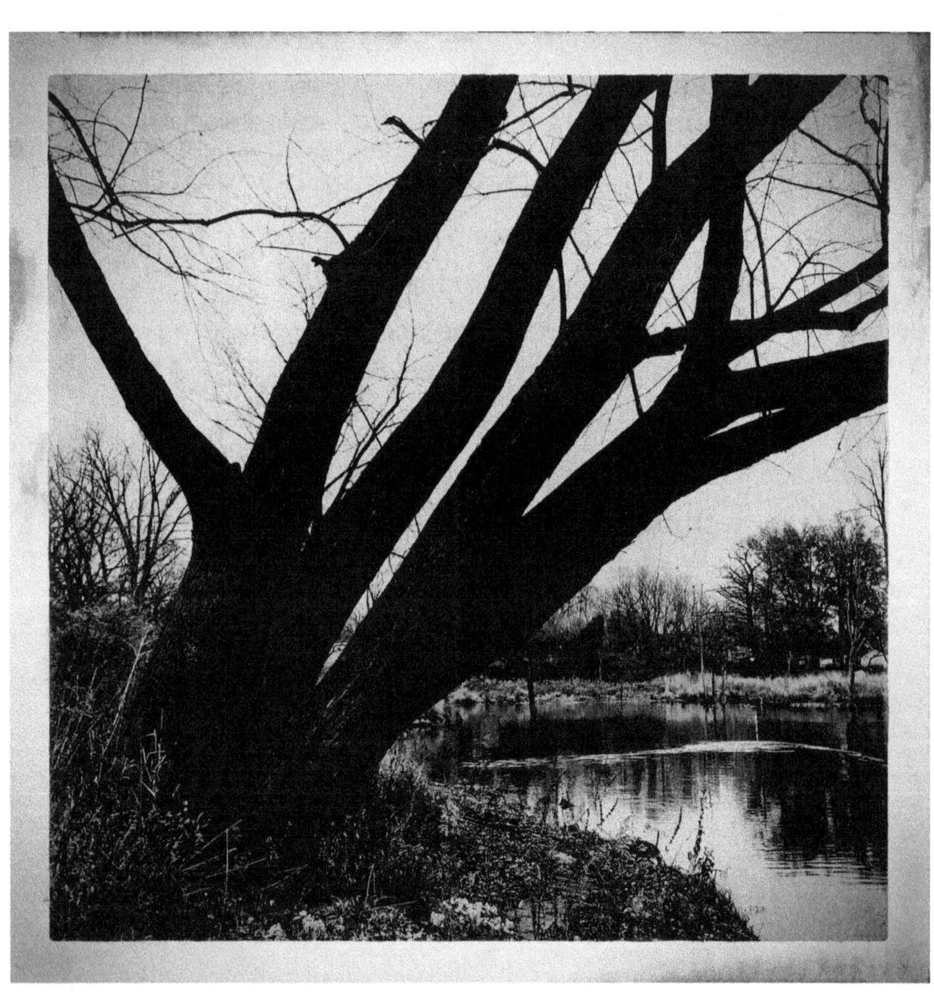

CHAGRIN RIVER, NORTHEASTERN OHIO

these bones settling
exactly into ice-age boulders
of Chagrin flow

on the dry boulder
just where I would next step,
a red dragonfly

back floating staring
at cumulus clouds floating,
this world floating

rock ringed fire pit,
oak sapling at center,
cool green flickerings

gnats flying past –
this life one separate click
of cicada's churr

bumblebee
legs so laden with pollen,
carrying two suns

Chagrin rush flows in
one ear out the other
so there is only river

O moon,
lightning bug
burns also now

looking up for moon –
it's floating next to me
on dark pond

grasping at minnows –
fingers an empty sieve
but for fish shit strand

just off the freeway
frog croaking assures it's not
the end of world yet

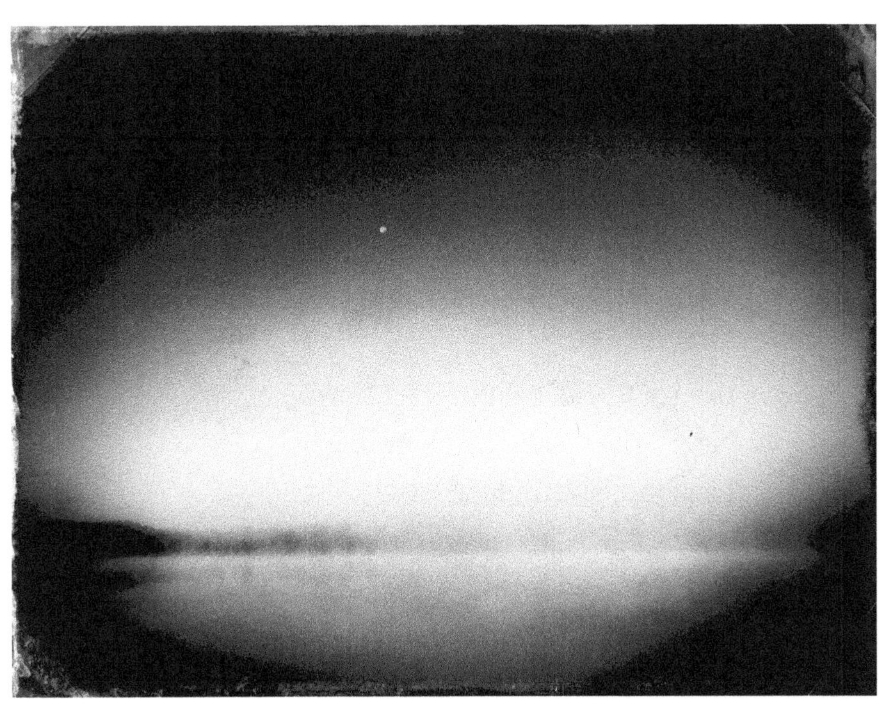

T H I R T Y - F I V E

NEW ORLEANS

freighter horn blows –
waking after Katrina,
Bywater home still here

honeybees buzzing
Greek wooden porch columns –
history's sweetness

dry rot Greek columns –
New Orleans always slumping
back into swampland

New Orleans scents –
crawfish boil, tabasco, stale beer –
clinging sweaty shirt

drunken frat boys
bargain Big Easy Sex
with sober drag queens

PORTSMOUTH, OHIO

rusty blue car sinking
under waves of ivy,
creeping window open

boarded up house –
backyard weeds grown head tall
over rusty swing set

rehab girl picks rose,
crushes petals and throws them
on cracked sidewalk

May storm blowing
Ohio river whitecaps –
voices of drowned slaves

rusty Kentucky plate
imprinted with butterfly,
yellow one flies by

SIDNEY, WESTERN OHIO

white bird droppings
glowing dusk trail —
full moon

bird songs at dusk –
no old folks left
to tell their names

red children's glove
stuck on oily pavement –
first warm spring day

April evening breeze
over corn furrow stubble,
empty swing sways

MAUI

eucalyptus scent –
my breath, trade winds
through upper branches

yellow wild flowers
swallowing rusty pick up truck –
Maui spring dawn

Maui lava rock –
3,000 miles from anywhere else,
sea and sky closer

drops of rain blatting
avocado leaves, drowning out
ticking clock

sunset filled raindrops
glistening lava rock –
first star appears

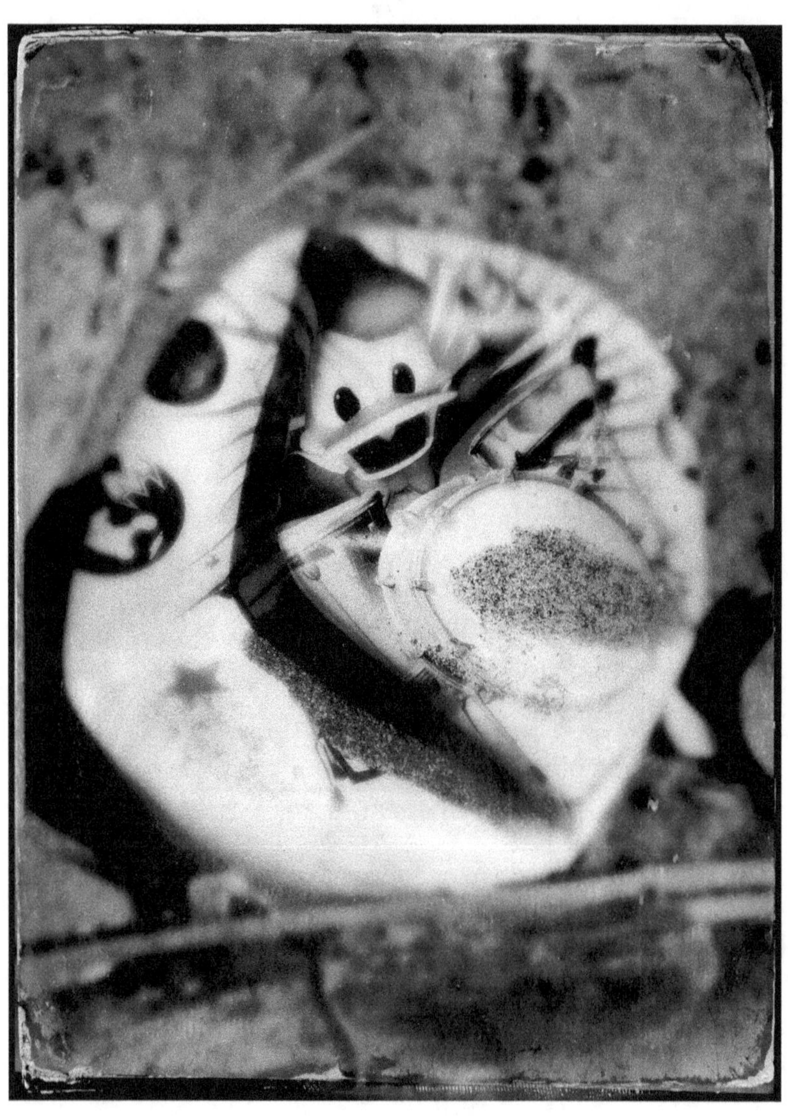

ZIONVILLE FARM
BOONE, NORTH CAROLINA

setting sun lights up
plastic beach ball stuck in creek –
earth 2017

once in a while a gong
sounds, no clock counts hours —
wind-blown world

trying to capture
last light dead leaf with photo –
these paltry words

wind gong tolls again —
if buddha statue hears,
he doesn't let on

koi school dark pond,
form Chinese character
floating beauty

ELSEWHERE IN AMERICA

Bowery subway –
hot ghost breaths of Irish navies
who dug this tunnel

Willie Mays glove at Hall,
how small, yet it caught the hopes
of all Cleveland

flock of cow pie pickers
swirl over a lone cow,
Texas goes on and on

Boulder dawn,
prairie dogs at their holes
beside new condos

NO TRESPASSING sign
Beside Flat Iron Trail,
land stolen from Utes

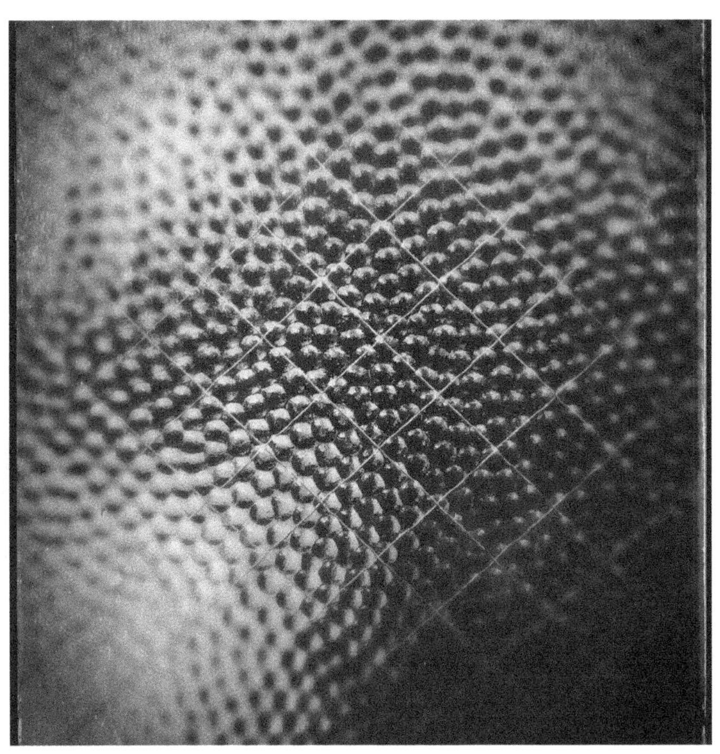

Vegas airport –
fatted calves are landing,
lost souls leaving

Lake Mead sucked up,
spit out in fountains of Vegas –
shiny slot coins spill

struggling up Aspen trail
an ant carrying a single wing –
iridescent death

stone head of Buddha
amid grey stone garden dawn –
all stones Buddha heads

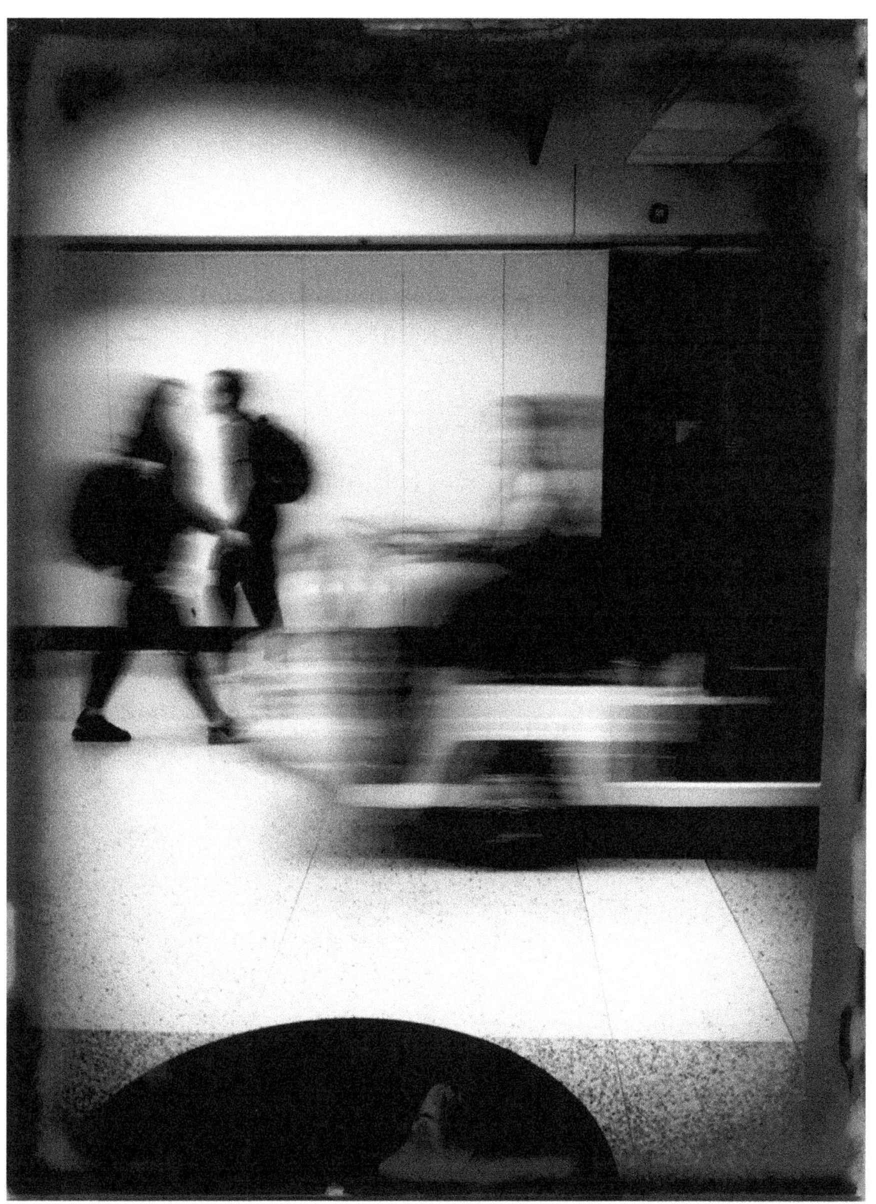

PORTLAND ZEN GARDEN

on back of stop sign
on way to Zen garden,
YOU ARE NOT WHAT YOU OWN

moss covered stone monk
meditating on side of trail –
I can't sit that still

fat slug climbs
on new shiny bamboo –
slimy calligraphy

leaving zen garden,
one dry leaf caught in web
above EXIT

PHILIPPINES

rainy day beach
between palms empty hammock swings —
not even your footprint

breeze whistles over
half empty beer bottle,
Guimaras isle time

driftwood carver
waited all through lunch
to sell us Jesus

Pinoy boys jumping
into the surf, soldier laughing,
his slung gun slips

peanut girl begs
Please sir, only ten pesos,
pouts then smiles

cocks crowing dawn
coconut trees swaying,
libido rising

Ilo Ilo city mall –
alongside new parking lot
water buffalo munches

fish skin to street cat,
bag of shrimp chips to beggar,
Emily's tears

Mimi answers Chang Tzu:
I know why the fish is happy,
it's not on my plate

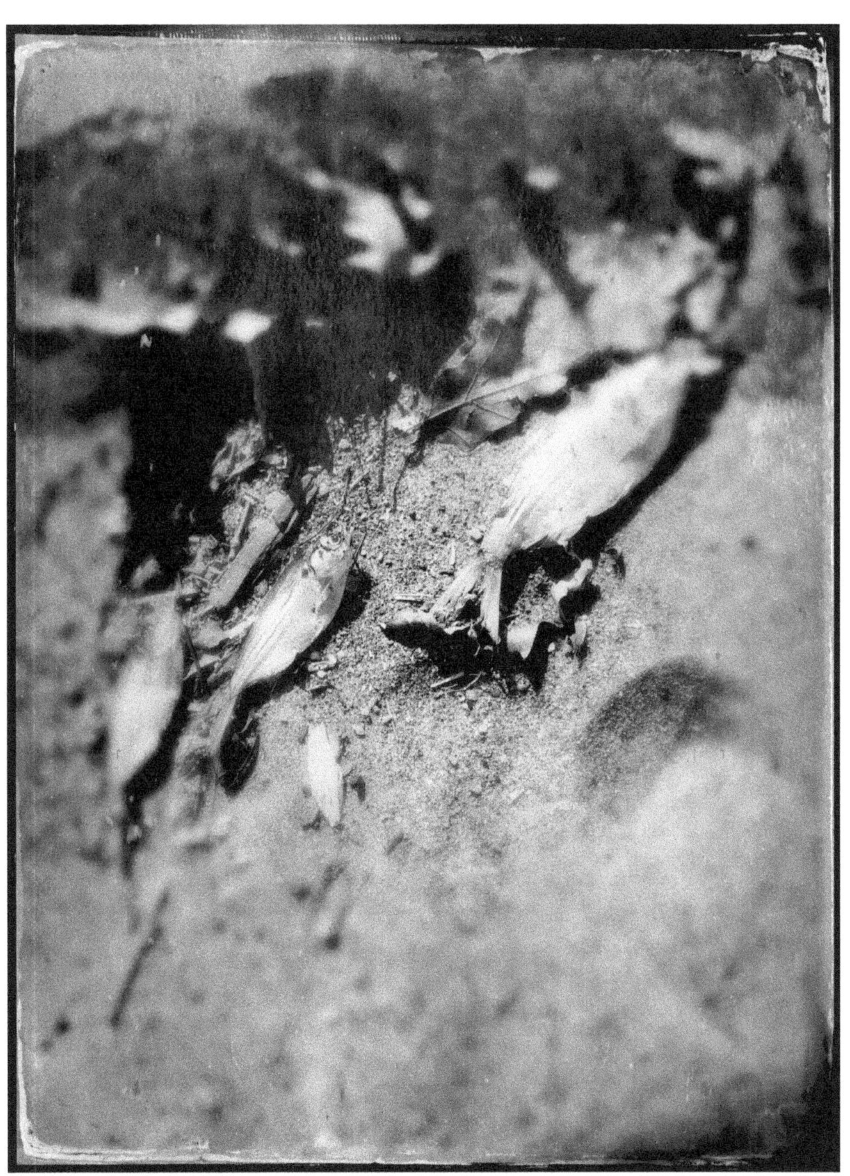

JAPAN

Nakano station –
amid flood of back and blue suits,
orange-haired head bobbing

all sakura fallen,
she gathers them in small hands,
opens them to breeze

crossing the Tama
April rain on train window –
Basho's last journey

Kamakura station –
last sakura
swirling cold puddle

through April downpour
friend's words murmured –
uguiso singing

Suzuki's grave –
wet webs on half dead maples,
cherry stem dancing

Yuki waving goodbye
at the station, still waving
as train pulls out of sight

hotel bed rocking,
thought it love-making
until earth settled

last night Nakano –
Flashing red lights on high-rises
Pink pouring moonrise.

if I hear anymore
about Japan's Sakura, my head
will explode blossoms

TANKA, TOKYO

From her small hands,
she unfurls cherry blossoms
over cold spring wind.
Gifts of delicate light
from her pale hands

Her plum kimono
same color as her lips
smiling in the cold;
not even 10,000 winters
could dim that smile.

The heat of her smile,
the monitor glows
binary hopes for visual.
If only words could fly
back into blue dusk sky.

HONG KONG

Bruce Lee bronze station
tenses on Hong Kong harbor –
high rises cower

Kowloon promenade
people fishing with hand lines –
Hong Kong skyline

Kowloon park pond
off Nathan Street sales' hubbub,
turtle paddling

Hong Kong peak no view,
but mall where you can buy
postcard of the city

Hong Kong's richest man
started on the street corner
selling plastic flowers

THAILAND

pale glow teak floor
calls to balcony, the moon
caught in spider's web

cave guide match,
gilt buddha flecks
filling empty footsteps

orange round beetle
on Green Mountain peak,
only monk here

boy throws rocks off peak
building another mountain
stone by stone

bamboo clatter –
skull whistling jazz
with summer breeze

Chang Mai to Bangkok train,
this seat making me sit
buddha straight all night

Bo tree at Wat Pho
next to reclining Buddha –
leaves flutter awake

cave museum cobwebs
on elephant skulls, headless buddhas —
no mind

Mai Sai billboard –
smiling young woman walks hand
in hand with pink condom

SINGAPORE

amid skyline of cranes,
HDB flats and rain-trees,
pagoda peak

in Singapore state
even the coke machine
knows my name

gazing at the moon
bit by mosquito,
round drop of blood

thank you mosquito
for reminding I'm in skin —
still alive

clicking of pen,
cricket's song,
one haiku

tembusa blossoms –
one more whiff
before I go inside

bare face moon
is no clock for love –
silver palm clatter

Singapore night –
exhaust from buses,
tembusa blossoms

trying to find quiet
middle of Singapore –
crickets don't care

stunned by stars –
brought back to earth
by cell phone tower

kid walks with grandpa
his squeaky first steps,
grandpa's last

Mondai Lake dawn mist –
cabbie at stop light gazing
across calm water

one butterfly flapping
across rush-hour freeway –
Singapore skyline

Hawker busboy
lived through Japanese occupation —
still wiping tables

Singapore's epitaph:
too busy working and shopping –
banana leaf curb

BKE freeway
goes round and round –
pursuit of happiness

TEMASEK (MALAYSIAN FOR SINGAPORE)

Temasek dusk —
frog trilling jungle
along freeway hurry

Temasek dusk —
jungle edge monkey stares
at freeway then back

Temasek dusk —
pink sunset on highrise,
poles of pink laundry

sadhu walking beach –
plastic bag of chai in one hand
cell phone in the other

one leaf floating
over koi pond school –
I am childless

koi hang still
till I toss a coin in –
don't need change

Singapore shower –
each afternoon at three
fat rain blossoms splat

pausing to feel
wall of cool air right before
warm rain waves

rush hour traffic roars
bougainville median
till red stop light

half the world's oil
ships through Mellaca straights –
dying sun sets

hiking the jungle
till Singapore hurry dissolves
into insect drone

BUKIT JUNGLE GINKO, SINGAPORE

Bukit jungle hike
centered with first few steps
then every step

Bukit jungle –
4:08, I check my phone
before time leaves

deeper in jungle,
risking dengue and soldiers
to sit naked

at quiet mound
empty tracks, empty flip flops,
walking stick laid down

mosquitos fly
through shadows, saving them harm,
I stay in the sun

isn't the mosquito
also going with its true flow
biting my arm?

BALI

Lemboyan seaweed
laid out on mats to dry —
soggy money

tethered cow
chewing cud of this world,
kind eyes staring

hunger in Bali –
even animal statues,
leave mouths open

Danny Boy in Bali
played by Indonesian bands,
tears in my Guinness

Nyepi on Bali –
quietest island on earth,
petals falling

FIRENZE

blue stage lights –
gnats hover microphone,
drunk on poetry

la prima stella brilla,
una scala de pesca argento
nuatto via

vesper bells ringing –
pigeons rising over
luminous Duomo

full moon dripping
rose petals over Roman wall –
Firenze dusk

Tuscan sunset –
on 2,000 year old wall,
my cracking shadow

PEREDELKINO, MOSCOW

pines pointing blue sky
over Yevtushenko's dacha –
no Moscow smog

breeze through birches,
Yevtushenko upstairs,
shuffling poems

through the closet door
of Zhenya's dacha gleams
an old samovar

over foldout bed
an angel icon blesses my pillow —
morning glows

last night at Zhenya's —
I sleep on the couch under
Pushkin's death mask

SENRYUS

Ken Kawaji says,
nothing lasts forever except
a poetry reading

practicing compassion
she hit him with a statue
of Buddha

Kerouac, we knock
your pickled bones together,
Tibetan be bop

sitting on hopper,
too depressed to even crap,
I don't give a shit

everything is holy –
especially the plop
of turd in toilet

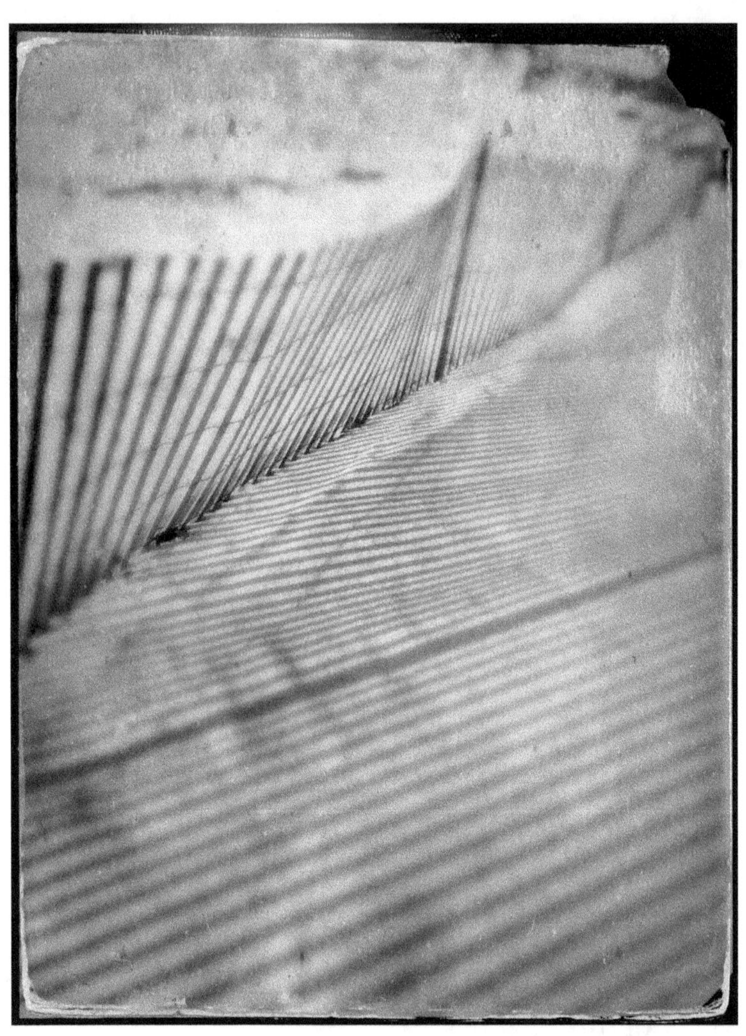

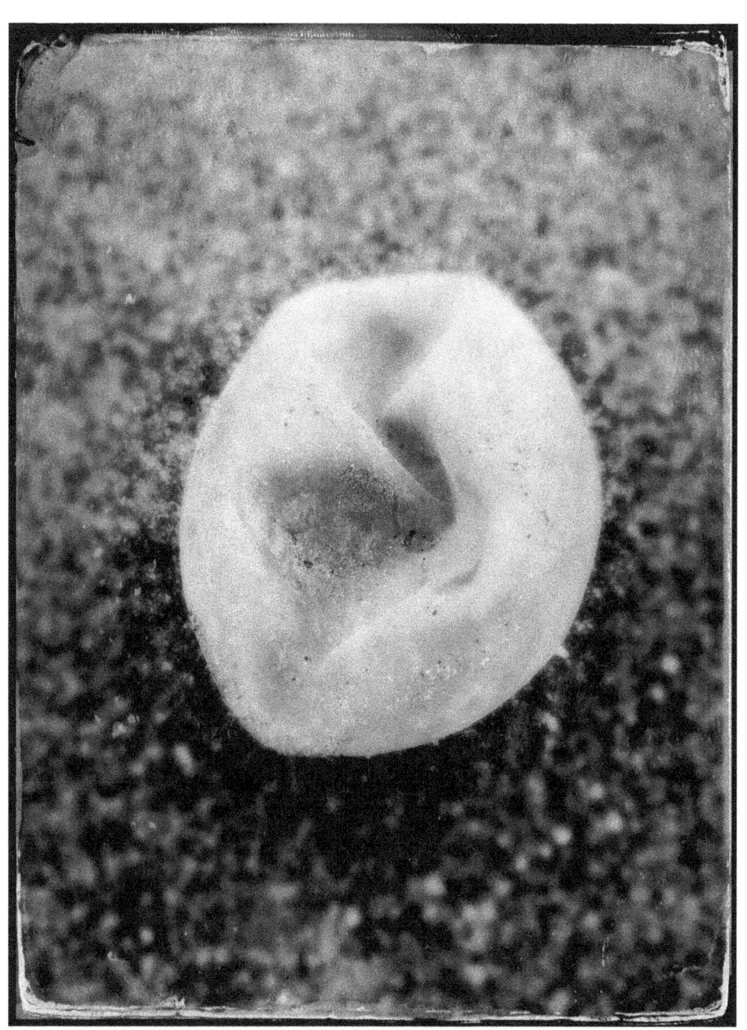

SIXTY-SEVEN

sound of one hand clapping
could be applause if two people
sit side by side

not even Buddha
can stop me from swatting
the fly from my thigh

cat lady gave
all forty cats a name – when she died,
they ate her

cardiologist dies
of heart attack at the podium
of cardiologist conference

rustling red oak leaves
fox squirrel leaping from branch to —
THUMP! even they miss

sometimes you must
get your ass kicked to get
your shit together

we're both old farts
but at least you are
four farts older

so go ahead and cry
a river but build a bridge
and get over it

cleaning the office
I find a faded article
"Cleaning Your Office"

Happy New Year!
no Mayan end of world —
back to work sucks

When I get depressed
I think about how long
I'm gonna be dead

dreamed I won
a million, by the time I woke
I didn't have a dime

what are your first words
on waking? Dalai Lama answers,
happy to be here

it will all work out
in the end – if it doesn't,
it's not the end

the problem with doing
nothing is never knowing
when you're done

Easter morning –
the tomb is empty, Jesus
has left the building

old man's advice,
don't trust a fart and
never waste a hard on

dying orange sun sinks
below Lake Erie's cold blue horizon —
another Brown's season

hillbilly's last words
hold my beer, watch this, I seen it
on a cartoon once

not poetry workshop,
a cognitive dissonance
integration session

not poetry workshop,
a drinking club with
a poetry problem.

Tried to sell me soul
but nobody was buying –
Put it on eBay, she says.

don't just do something
sit still, bumper sticker reads
stuck in traffic jam

opposable thumb –
evolution comes down to
TV remote buttons

don't play hoops with monks
from Tibet, their robes too long –
can't tell where feet go

today's headline —
HORRIFIC CRASH, WORST EVER SEEN,
FAN HAS VIDEO

middle age man, ass
migrates to gut, belly sticks out
more than dicky doo

I hate clowns —
when I was a boy I thought
they would blow up

bullcrap ain't out
of the hole too long before
flies are on it

truck full of chickens,
dirty feathers splay rusty cages,
drives past golden arches

monkey mind
swings from branch to branch
chasing bananas

sound of one hand clapping –
sound of two hands clapping
dead mosquito

his car broke down,
repo'ed — owns nothing now
but his debt

freedom is knowing
when you get to the fork in the road
you're screwed either way

they cut down the last
Florida white pine — what
did they make, a coffin?

“EVERY POEM A DEATH POEM” BASHO

every haiku
a death poem, every breath
could be your last

driving late for work,
held up by a funeral,
I pull in behind

on Uncle Frankie’s arms,
bruises where Death tapped him
asking for the time

from her deathbed, Ma says,
move the flowers from the sill,
I want to see the sky

Cleaning dead people
from his cell phone he tells me,
Your Mom was in there

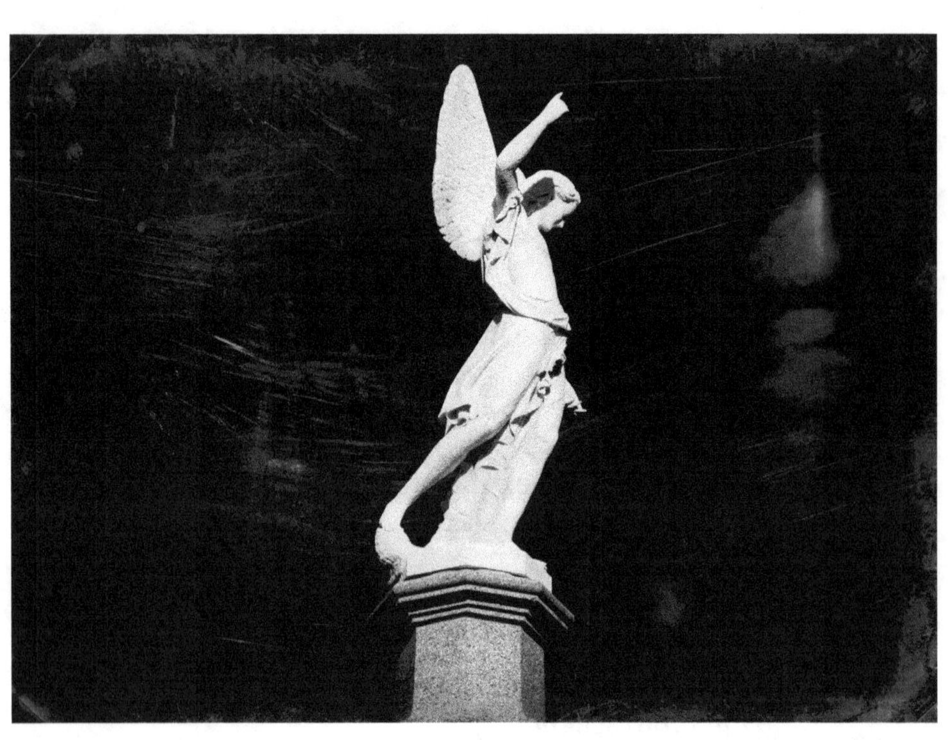

outside cemetery,
roadwork so everyone can
get to work on time

my mom can't speak,
trach tube clogged with blood,
she mouths, *goodbye*

she reads obituaries,
only time friends are in the paper
is when they die

cemetery mosquito,
belly swelling red
from my living hand

key found in graveyard –
what door could it open here
or anywhere?

spider, web centered,
eight shiny eyes, hairy fangs –
you too will die

only this birth right,
breath to give away,
hello, farewell

leopard frog leaps
wary of heron, I wait
bony tap on shoulder

heron track runes
ancient runes tells life
is patient deadly

the first man to walk
on the moon has died —
footprint still up there

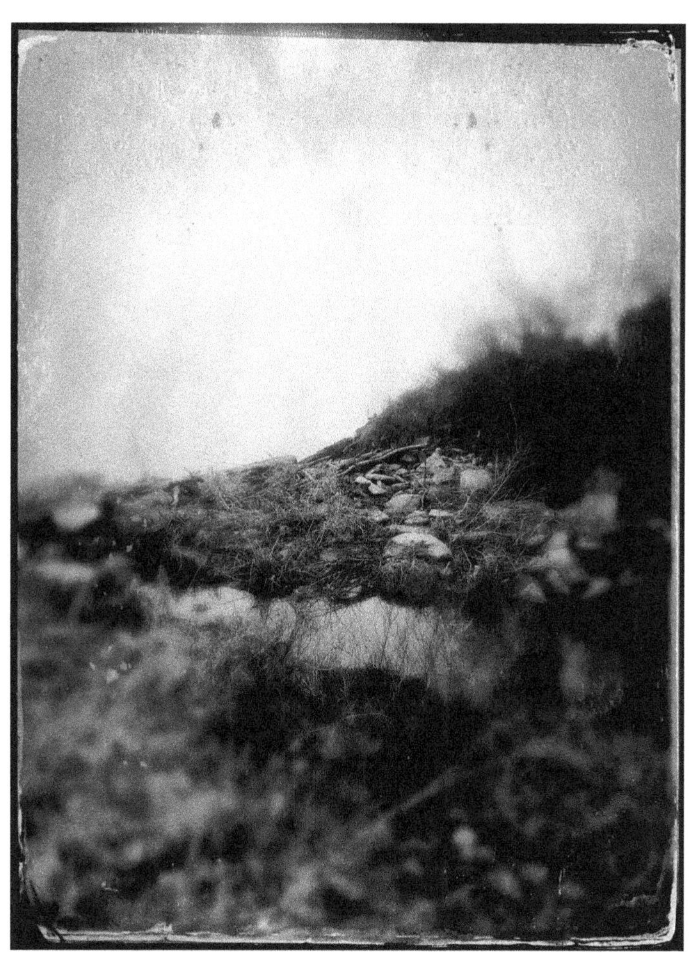

I'll just wander off
into San Cristobel desert –
these bones final haiku

bare March woodlands –
some trees hold onto others
long after they're dead

first poem written
on a sympathy card, slid
into Dad's casket

my father's stubble
found in old electric razor
after his death, still black

In Memoriam, Cornelia…
can't make out the rest,
we all become blank

cemetery grass,
torn price tag, $1.19 –
what it costs to live

mulberry tree growing
out of locked tomb,
juice stains on stones

my living shadow
does not cast as long a shadow
as Mary's tombstone

bird crap dribbled
down decaying tombstone
dead wish they could see

it takes one's whole life
to finally learn by heart
the beat of death

gravestones — dead would give
anything to hear dry leaves
crunching underfoot

cracking skeleton —
this bridge that carries flesh
from birth to death

smile at hungry ghost
smiling back from mirror every day —
you've never been here

face of tombstone
worn off blank grey —
our original face

upstairs they sit
in offices facing the graveyard
not the ball park

pointing bony finger
Don't EVER forget- life goes
through you, not to you

spray of red speckles
across the get well card,
one of Ma's last breaths

plastic bottle on shore
of Lake Erie will outlast
my dying mother

showing you,
as I waved goodbye,
the bones of my hand

life is a life sentence,
imprisoned by skeleton,
breath's key sets one free

wherever I cycle
in Key West I end up at
the cemetery

I find a carcass
seething with maggots —
even death wants sex

wet webs shimmering
over cemetery lawn –
October sunset

used to be dead
the whole year, but now i'm dead
one day at a time

better to do it
than not do it, put that
on my tombstone

I'll never retire,
I'll be digging my own grave
the rest of my days

everyday I breathe
deeper — one day it will be
all exhale

between bright star
and atom inside, I spin –
breath burns away

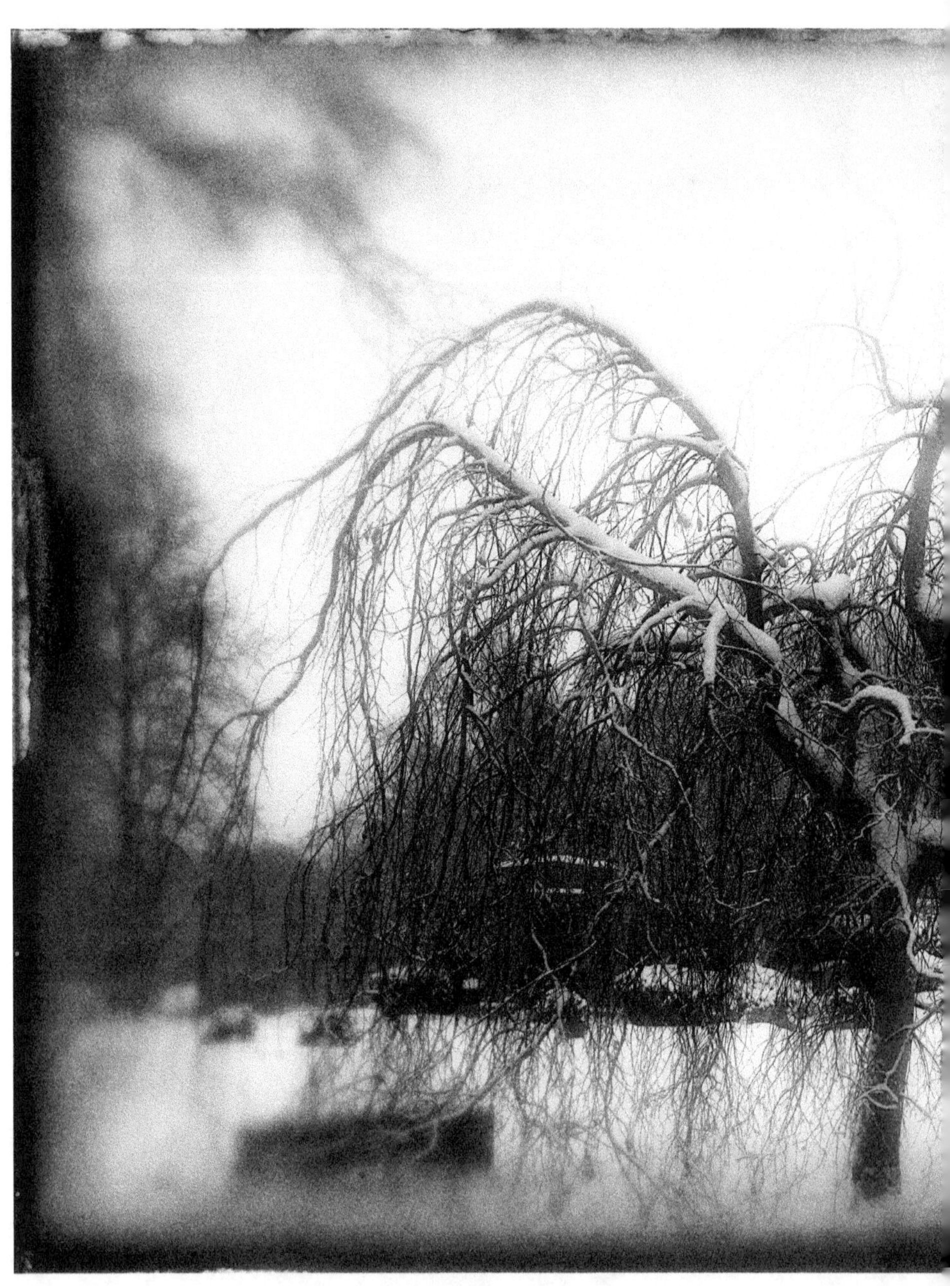

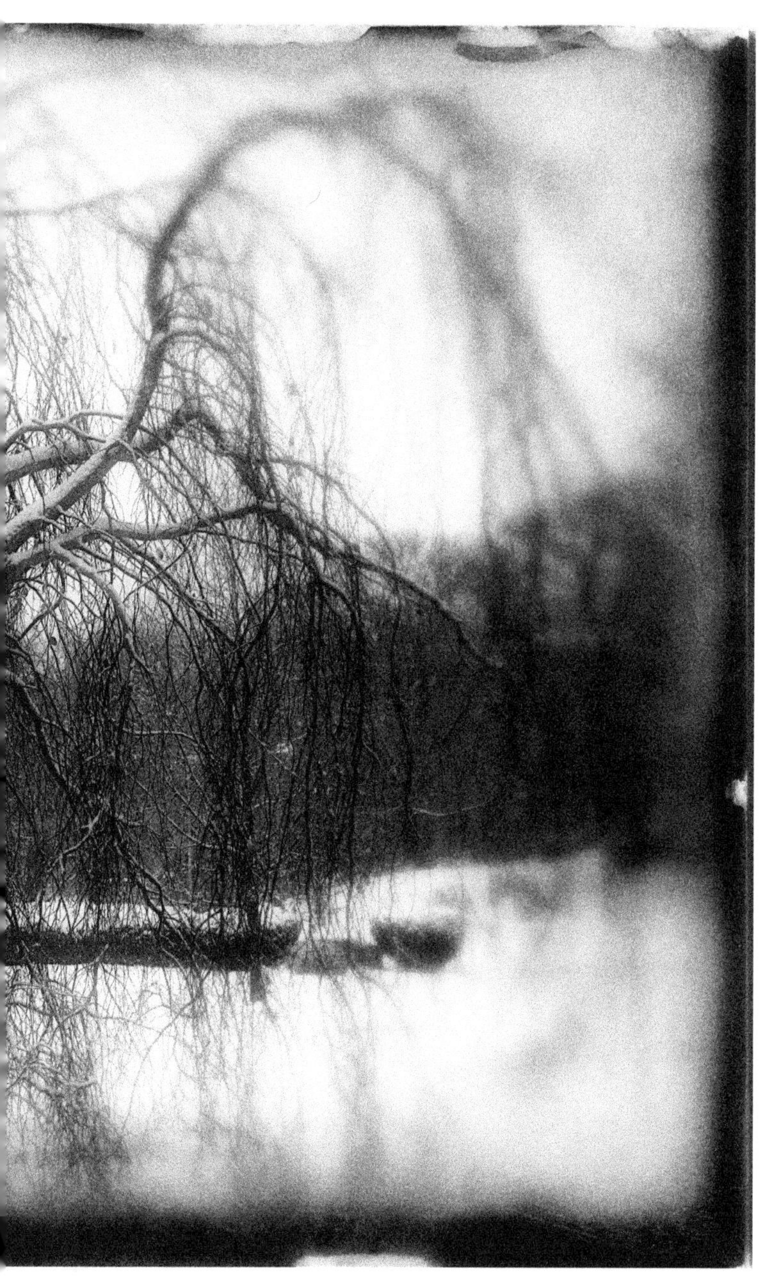

PLOP! THE HAIKU MOMENT

One of the origin stories for Basho's legendary frog pond haiku comes from DT Suzuki. He depicts a dialogue between Basho, who began practicing Zen in the later stages of his writing career, and Buccho, his monk mentor: Buccho asks, *How are you?*

Basho replies, *the moss has grown greener since the rain.*

Buccho's query continues, *what zen there before moss was greener?*

Basho answers:

old pond,
frog jumps into
plop!

There are other versions of the genesis of that simple splash koan. Koh-ko, poet friend from Singapore sojourn, tells *there were a bunch of monks at the pond, drinking probably,* (he sipped a beer), *and Basho was advising them not to write poems about dragons in the sky...*

— *You mean mythological creatures?* I asked, sensing it sounded like Koh-ko's continuous critique debunking the influence of mainland Chinese culture. He is also an outsider from his own mother culture, being Ho-Kein, Singapore Chinese, so we found a common outsider perspective.

— *Yes, not dragons in the sky but frogs in the pond.* Koh was positing Basho as a proponent of the ordinary. Of course, that is the basis of Zen. Another account, and this may be were Koh's version comes from, has a group of Basho's disciples sitting in the hut they built for him, listening to spring rain and frogs intermittantly jumping in the pond. Basho wrote the last two lines first:

a frog jumps in —
sound of water

A student suggests a traditional kigo, "golden kerria", a flower as the first line. Basho rejected it and went with the plain, ordinary "old pond" subverting the classical tradition in favor of the actual. Not suprising, in his later writing, he suggest that if you want to know about the pine, go to the pine. That being said, the dictate that haiku must be factual to the actual experience, contrasts with another of Basho's composition tips— that lines must be tested on the tongue over and over. Apparantly he rewrote many of his haiku, some over years. So, the spontaneous overflow of emotion can be recollected in tranquility. Does he contradict himself? He contains multitudes, to paraphrase Whitman.

But we weren't there. Maybe they were composing a renku together and all other haikus dissolved, fireflies in the dusk.

Anyway, we're here. Now the way I see it, Basho is standing at pond's edge alongside his mentor, silence between them, as he gazes into stillness from still center of his own being, shifts his weight, rustling his robe — it was dusk of a cool spring evening — ever so slightly, that shift felt from marshy land around water's edge — after all it is "an old pond" —and the frog, who was also meditating and embodying survival instinct as well — the same instinct that moves Basho — well, that instinct kicks in and here goes that green blur stretched out over ancient pond quietude mediatating stillness mirroring still sky, pause between breaths, all brought together into, wait for it...

plop! ("sound of water")

Ink circle enso opening, universe and void simultaneously rippling outwards, empty heart sutra ringing: form is emptiness, emptiness is form. Still.

The instructor at the writing workshop Kohko and I attended that day said there are no perfect circles in nature. Extrapolating, if the enso weren't somewhat asymmetrical it would not move – that shift of foot prompting the frog plop. The essence of zen is...*is!* That simple pivot of form *is* emptiness, emptiness *is* form. It's a verb – that splash in the pond Basho experienced, that moment, 'the sound of water' as it is often translated from the Japanese, and just after. Moments blossom, wither, bloom again. Moments break through the surface reality. We awaken with them, in them, through them, in the unity of the holy spirit, as childhood Catholic litany echoes, which I repeat to Koh-ko, prompting an aesthetic leap via Keats, *truth is beauty, beauty is truth* rejoined by *death is the mother of beauty,* as Wallace Stevens poemed. *Every haiku is a death poem*, Basho said.

The silence before, the silence after, the silence at the heart of the heart sutra, the systole diastole, the *is* between, dark matter potential, god particle. What does silence do? Silence is. I quote the haiku I had composed the day before in response to one of the St Nick's students asking,

are rocks living things?
sit bones on boulder thinking —
no mind

To which the student responded, that's so cheem, which means, in Singlish, "deep." And her friend added, *Cheem along lah*. What's that, I asked? *The study of deepness.*

The essence of zen is...*is*, I said to Koh. That splash: sound frog light water splash unified field theory proved...*plop!* I explained how I took the students to the Koi pond and prepped them by saying, I'll recite the most famous haiku of all time.

ancient pond,
frog jumps in
sound of water.

I actually just made the sound, *splash*, without an exclamation mark.

That's it ! ? one blurted. Quizzical looks all around. I repeated it. It's not a trick. It won't be on the dreaded national English test. That's it. This is it! Seek no farther. Right here now. That meeting between human and nature, simply be. And yet entire shelves of libraries have been filled by scholarship extrapolating this one small haiku.

Later, when we were reading our haiku to each other in the drama room, I had them respond with *A-ha*, as in the A-ha moment, that epiphany when it all becomes clear, an exclamation that umbrellas all haiku moments. That insight turned outsight. They took to that, akin to Singlish slang, *lah*. I extrapolated with other exclamations to represent different moods, those interstices where human nature and nature merge such as *ew* to represent disgusting beauty, or *ow* for painful awareness, or *wow*, for stunned moments, or *aww* for endearing or delightful moments, or *huh?* for perplexingly true moments, or *eh* for resigned moments, or *oh*, for surprisingly deep moments. These vowel sounds represent a simple way to introduce the traditional four moods of haiku: *Sabi*, quiescent detachment, *Wabi*, recognition of the such ness of ordinary things; *Aware*, the resonance of transience, (that all things pass back into the formless void from whence they came) and *Yugen*, the mystery of things suddenly made clear. And although haiku in American English rarely heed this awareness of moods, it is still a place to understand from whence classic Japanese haiku issue. I offered some of my efforts:

floating Koi,
coins in fountain pool –
two bucks worth

koi hang still
silver coin flutters down —
green moss glow

Egrets flapping
so high —
spring clouds

I explained the microcosm moment reflects the macrocosm. That one swirl tip of a fractal contains all fractals of the big picture. *That's so cheem.*

Or, as is often said about the last line of Basho's frog pond, *Untranslatable.*

I relate this story to Koh-Ko and I rap my knuckles on the table, then *ting, ting,* chopsticks on chrome table legs. Doesn't exist.

What do you mean? Koh harrumphs.
In the span of time, no, it doesn't exist. Form is emptiness, emptiness is form. Do rocks live? Yes, slowly. They breath ever so slowly, like the sun, which gives instantly light.

The pond is a mirror, reflecting whatever we see. Basho standing in the reflection, smiles.

Other monks around? Or is he alone?

Did a kid run up to the pond? Fifteen frogs would have jumped in.

That aptly describes good writing, he adds, *the combination of imagery and narrative.* But haiku eschew narrative.

It doesn't matter what spirituality you practice. The image creates a scene. You, the reader, decide what scene.

I say, the pond is on the page. The listener enters the silence, breaks the surface. Basho's frog sinks to the bottom, sees the world as a bubble burped, bursting the mirror of the surface, sees Basho's shape wavering there, smiling on the other side of silence. All can see a reflection in that pond from their own perspective, their own flawed, or heron keen, or nearsighted poet's vision, angle. But what we see is not words on a page but the image. Imagery tells the fable. No human being can steer it. Our words make merely the medium for imagination.

Koh-Ko agreed, criticizing a local poet for being too self-referential, expressing only the ego-involved theme of identity, as a kind of masturbation—

not a connection to the larger orgasm of the cosmos, I offered.

Koh-Ko frowns then suggests that the frog's jump is pure reflex like the butterfly effect. It's up to the reader to speculate the reason, their own interpretation of the poem.

Maybe it was Basho taking one more step, trying to get closer to the silence, a mistake (He might have fallen in, startled so), a happy accident.

Koh-Ko interjects, *there are no mistakes.*
Yes, buddhist dharma, there are none. Frog jumps, that verb, brings him back to focus, to catch his breath, experiencing the still point between inhale and exhale, the "is" of form is emptiness, emptiness is form, the nothing that is not there and the nothing that *is*, to quote Wallace Stevens again.

Poets are keen that the basis of their art is silence, the space around the words. They are adepts at respecting the great void from which all forms issue, the emptiness at the heart of sound, at the heart of the heart. Is it particle or wave? Yes!

How to translate that last line, the sound of water? *Splash*? That's the point, one can't explain it in that moment. It's a seed moment, blossom from silent void, expanding. *One thought fills immensity,* Blake said.

How much does a thought weigh? OM. That vibration. How can we tell the particle from the wave? We live in the moment between inhaling the future and exhaling the past. Let's go again to that pond, that moment's splash, rippling, contracting, as does breath. Change is the constant of time: life is *beautiful, suffering and transient.* Basho's breath I echo now, into sound of... Plop!

Furuike ya
kawazu tobikomu
mizu no oto

— Basho

Literal Translation

Fu-ru (old) i-ke (pond) ya,
ka-wa-zu (frog) to-bi-ko-mu (jumping into)
mi-zu (water) no o-to (sound)

The old pond--
a frog jumps in,
sound of water.

or more simply into.....plop

or into...*kerplunk* as Ginsburg translated.

Anyway, the onomatopoeic particle for "the sound of water" *oto*, echoes that interpretation. Each word of this haiku is simple in keeping with Basho's effort to speak in common language, as did Wordsworth and Whitman in English, each word carrying so much weight – heavy meaning.

Old pond might mean "mature," experienced, as in no longer a novice monk, and it has also been translated as ancient, alluding to the buddhist wisdom tradition;

pond references, by traditional association, to meditation, zazen;

frog (kawazu) actually refers to the archaic word for it, a nod to the tradition, mixed with colloquial speech and so his mentor would get the joke that he is actually parodying the assumption of seasonal words and their connotations, giving a nod to tradition and upending it at the same time since the standard usage of frog at that time was a sound marker for "spring," for song, for sexual longing, for romance akin to certain specific words for warblers. In fact, Japanese of this era could imitate dozens of different frog songs as well as bird songs.

But no romance for Basho and Buccho, these two old farts, now.

I envision them actually pond side, on a ginkgo (haiku hike), respecting haiku tenet that the poem be composed on the spot in the here and now, (hence the use of present tense for the form) not this immediate spontaneous overflow recollected later in tranquility, (doubtful they would get that excited about it, they've seen it all — but, ah, one is never too old for satori).

So, as Basho contemplates, the frog jumps into the sound of "plop" not just the breaking the surface of quietude, of buddhist tradition, but by breaking the speed of sound and light into silence, into the void.

In his autobiography, Allan Watts tells a story of an unorthodox drama teacher who used a zen approach to get actors to live in the moment, teaching people 'get with it,' where 'it' designates the world of nonverbal happenings which we usually call the physical or material world, without realizing these words are loaded with philosophical prejudice. The sound of a frog jumping into an old pond is 'Plop!' This 'Plop' isn't a philosophical category. 'Plop!' is just 'Plop!' This is the simplest thing in the world but the hardest to explain. If you understand it you can see that this 'Plop!' is all-of-a-piece with a thousand galaxies.

Buddha, remember, did not stay in that quietude, he practiced what all bodhisattva's must do once awake — bring satori into every day, go out into the world, hear the frog sing in spring or not, hear the simple *plop*, effortless, with no cause, no dharma drama, ringing outward to stillness, the world is sound, vibration, the frog's plop ringing stillness.

Haiku issue from this *suchness*, the ordinary mind, the simply human. What could be a more present way of living than performance, to be present in the present with your presence, perceiving and expressing simultaneously? The ego steps aside or is accepted into the mix as a necessary incumbrance. Chuang-Tzu describes it thusly, "the state in which ego and non-ego are no longer opposed is called 'the pivot of Tao.'

Indeed, my own arrival at haiku as zen meditation, a kind of spiritual GPS, came by way of Taoism, specifically in co-translating, with Julia Lin, Tang dynasty lyric poetry, particularly Wang Wei, the Ch'an (Taoist) Buddhist monk, while studying at Ohio University.

But this understanding is not alien to Western thought. Hippocrates notes (in his treatise on alimentation no less),

There is a common flow, one common breathing, all things are in sympathy. The whole organism and each of its parts are working in conjunction for the same purpose...the great principal extends to the extremist part, and from the extremist part it returns to the great principal, the one nature, being and not being.

Present in the present tense, your essence less tensely flows with knowing this ordinary world is full of so much sense it's nonsense. For a single cell, that small semipermeable membrane, is only a thin bubble between universal consciousness and floats so translucently it appears empty and indeed is — as breath is! *Plop*! So we sit zazen and respect the simply deep unconscious act of breathing being. I look out from where I sit on the riverbank during a ginkgo,

turning to look
for my friend downriver —
spider strand wind

child digging channels
in river bank sand —
rapid bubbles bursting

That last haiku is how the preceding exposition of being present, the sense of presence, came to me. Play is the child's work. The tick of the clock, the hours of contained time, does not interfere. "The hours of folly are measured by the clock. The Hours of wisdom no clock can measure." Blake said. Adults stay on the clock out of necessity and so miss the moment constantly. The haiku presence is akin to Whitman's "A child went forth and everything he looked upon he became." To see but also to be the sight at that moment, express it so that the words make a hologram. Of course, that's based on technology, clumsy approximation of reality. It's about seeing the "white flake of snow on the horses' mane," lofting up in the wind that creates the entire scene, image on image, collages it, but breathed in and out as words. This presents a fractal, microcosm that is an exact replica of the macrocosm as in Basho's

on a barren branch
the raven has perched
autumn dusk

where the arm of the swirl, the very tip of it, the crow and the branch as one, reveals the entire swirling arm of the cosmos and it's passing into darkness, the little reflected light of earth on the edge of this pin-wheel galaxy swirling through the dark, that a-ha moment whooshes out into the entire cosmos — as Blake said, "one thought fills immensity.'

The feeling that comes from the thing itself, unity of it, as ego steps aside or steps, unified with non-being, into the moment fully. Yet the past can be brought into the present tense of haiku, in the poignancy of what passes. Such as this haiku by Issa, amplified by his personal history of child loss —

heat shimmer
lingering in the eye,
a laughing face.

where his past and present overlap.

or Basho's historical haiku,

Ah! Summer grasses!
All that remains
Of the warriors' dreams

(Translated by: R. H. Blyth, 1952)

But haiku are more than just word pictures, snapshots of the present: They are not about capturing a scene, but releasing it. This is it! Pay attention to *is!* For if we do, compassion follows inevitably. Wordsworth's short introductory poem to Ode; Intimations of Immortality expresses the zen aesthetic of *suffering, contingency and transience.* Awake in that childlike wonder wandering reality,

My heart leaps up when I behold
A Rainbow in the sky:
So was it when my life began;
So is it now I am a Man;
So be it when I shall grow old,
Or let me die!
The Child is Father of the Man;
And I could wish my days to be
Bound each to each by natural piety.

Exactly,

Dali Lama was asked,
what is your first thought on waking?
happy to be here!

We should be leaping for joy everyday, "happy to be here!" But, as Thoreau advised, "We must learn to reawaken and keep ourselves awake, not by mechanical aids, but by an infinite expectation of the dawn, ..." Instead, *we gotta getta cuppa coffee, gotta go to work,* sullen cuz our team lost the game last night. We're dragged back to the past by regrets or into the future by worry, not being present, but always living ahead or behind ourselves. Self is the problem; it sees the world as a reflection of its thoughts. Indeed it is — to a certain extent. Haiku hike once a day to connect with ultimate reality, deep consciousness. *Forest bathing*, as it is called in Japan. We are not the only ones to ever have worries, to ever have eyeballs, to ever have a name. We are taught ego early on, how to protect it, dress it up, parade it around. And don't think the ascetic in his robe more zen than thou is not also a player projecting. So what is essence? Breath, the air which is what we share which, when we compose haiku, "gives to airy nothing a local habitation and a name." Yes, earth of bones, fire of flesh, water of blood and air of breath upon which we sit, balanced,

this morning I breath
deeply this haiku —
all exhale

Poems begin in silence and end in silence. Zen is finally silent. Once you open your mouth you've already blown it, trying to discern, dissect, or designate. That is the paradox. And why Buddha's great sutra was simply holding out a lotus blossom. And why Basho said, every poem is a death poem. The frog's plop and just after.

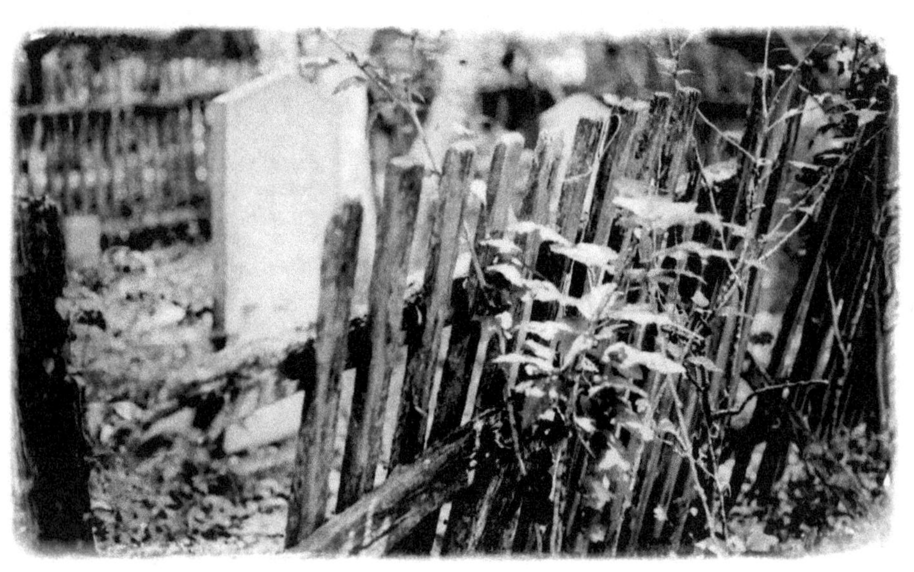

www.ingramcontent.com/pod-product-compliance
Lightning Source LLC
LaVergne TN
LVHW010628100826
845148LV00014B/3156
* 9 7 8 1 7 3 2 5 5 1 4 3 5 *